W9-DGE-713

Bina Agarwal

Beyond Family Farming: Gendering the Collective

19 Novembre 2019, Accademia Nazionale dei Lincei, Rome

Fondazione
Internazionale Balzan
"Premio"

Accademia Nazionale dei Lincei

akademien der wissenschaften schweiz
académies suisses des sciences
accademie svizzere delle scienze
academias svizras da las scienzas
swiss academies of arts and sciences

THE ANNUAL BALZAN LECTURE

10

BEYOND FAMILY FARMING: GENDERING THE COLLECTIVE

by

BINA AGARWAL

2017 Balzan Prizewinner

LEO S. OLSCHKI

2021

ISBN 978 88 222 6738 2

CONTENTS

List of Balzan Prizewinners:

ENRICO DECLEVA

President of the International Balzan Foundation "Prize"

WELCOME ADDRESS

In these times marked by the intensification of economic inequality on a global level, with its visible, painful effects like mass migration and the re-emergence of nationalism and intolerance, it would be a good opportunity to stop and think about possible responses that might come from those who study the underlying dynamics of these phenomena. One is gender inequality, which is surely not only characteristic of developing countries, but which also persists in different forms in the so-called wealthy countries.

This desire for going into greater depth on the problem became more concrete when the General Prize Committee of the Balzan Foundation, perfectly attuned to the spirit of our times, decided to include gender studies among the subject areas for the Balzan Prizes in 2017, and to award that prize to a developmental economist, Bina Agarwal, with the following motivation: *For challenging established premises in economics and the social sciences by using an innovative gender perspective; for enhancing the visibility and empowerment of rural women in the Global South; for opening new intellectual and political pathways in key areas of gender and development.*

Ever since the beginning of her intense career, Bina Agarwal has always been interested in searching for useful ways to change the lives of women in the poor rural areas of India and, more generally speaking, in the Global South, a subject that today is as relevant as it is inadequately understood. By raising new questions and following a truly interdisciplinary route that joins economics, law, ethnography, sociology, political science and anthropology, she has arrived at original insights and answers. And these answers have not only opened up an agenda of academic research around the world, they have also influenced government policy, NGOs and international agencies at work in eliminating gender inequality in all of its forms.

Today I have the honour and the privilege of listening to a lecture that I am sure will be interesting and original, and I do not want to take any more time away from it.

Please just allow me to end with my thanks first of all to Professor Agarwal for accepting our invitation, and secondly to the Accademia Nazionale dei Lincei for being our host in its prestigious headquarters. Together with the Swiss Academies of Arts and Sciences and the Balzan Foundation, the Lincei is part of joint agreements for collaboration. Professor Quadrio-Curzio, President Emeritus of the Lincei, is also President of this Joint Commission, and in extending my greetings and thanks for his constant commitment and dedication, I leave him the floor.

PRESENTATION OF BINA AGARWAL
BY ALBERTO QUADRIO-CURZIO

Vice President of the International Balzan Foundation "Prize",
President Emeritus of the Accademia Nazionale dei Lincei,
President of the Joint Commission Balzan-Lincei-Swiss Academies

Thank you, President Decleva, for addressing such kind, friendly words to me, and for your constant attention to the Accademia dei Lincei and matters it is sensitive to. This has been demonstrated by your presentation today, where you mention that the contribution of Bina Agarwal truly represents a *unicum* in what we might define as the social sciences, or "humanities with strong socio-economic content", and of course in the fields of political economy and economic development.

Although I probably met Bina Agarwal many years ago at the University of Cambridge, and was already very familiar with her work, I got to know her better when, in Argentina in 1999, she joined the Executive Committee of the International Economic Association (IEA), and later in 2002 became its Vice President. I do not think that, before her, any other woman political economist had ever been elected to this important position. Her election was even more important since her research could not be placed in the realm of mainstream economics which, at that time, was dominant in the IEA.

In fact, Bina Agarwal's work truly expresses what can be called political economy, in the outstanding tradition of the most influential classical economists, and in a field that had not been studied as deeply or carefully by most economists, that is, gender inequalities in economic and social development.

Among her many works, I would like to mention one which represents a clear turning point in studies on gender inequality: *A Field of One's Own*, published by Cambridge University Press in 1994. This book, which focuses on gender inequalities in property and land in five countries, will always stand out in the history of political economy for its originality of thought, its methodology and insights, and its courage.

As regards method, in this and in her vast body of other research, Bina Agarwal combines the rigour of objective analysis of official statistical data with direct in-depth field observation, to confirm results and enrich their meaning. Hence, she has not just provided original ideas, but she has demonstrated their validity through data analysis and field research. This has involved very hard work – I would say almost heroic work – because fieldwork is never easy, and on this sensitive subject carries considerable risk.

With regard to results, beyond scientific understanding she brought to light a situation of profound injustice and discrimination toward women. She also pointed out the negative effects that such discrimination has had, and continues to have, on a country's economic, social and human development, and especially on the rural environment. In one set of research results, she demonstrated the many aspects of vulnerability in women's lives in LDCs, for example, the deadly health effects on women, such as acute upper respiratory infections and even cancer, due to indoor air pollution caused by cooking with unprocessed biofuels.

As regards courage, Bina Agarwal used her deep understanding of inheritance laws to undertake specific political action – a campaign to pressure the Indian Parliament to change laws that discriminated against women. She was successful, and in 2005 India changed its inheritance law for Hindus, removing the discriminatory clauses that prevented women from inheriting joint family property and agricultural land.

Over the years, Bina Agarwal's research has also succeeded in proving that women, when placed on the same plane as men, be it in farming or in community institutions, enable significantly better outcomes, such as in the productivity of land and in forest conservation. Women raise the pool of knowledge and skills and bring to the economy and society special resources and gender complementarity.

One final observation. In Agenda 2030 of the Sustainable Development Goals (but partially even in the Millennium Development Goals), Goal 5 emphasises women's land rights, making it clear that this is one of the crucial elements for overcoming underdevelopment as well as discrimination against women. I believe that this target in

Goal 5 was influenced by the enormous impact of Bina Agarwal's original work on the subject.

For all these reasons, I am very pleased that Agarwal will deliver this Annual Balzan Lecture. As you know, she won the 2017 International Balzan Prize for Gender Studies, but I am pleased to add that she is also a fellow of the Accademia dei Lincei and a co-editor of *Economica Politica: Journal of Analytical and Institutional Economics*, published by Springer and il Mulino. You will be delighted to hear that il Mulino will be publishing a selection of her essays, thus bringing to wider Italian audiences greater knowledge of her contributions to economic and social development.

LECTURE BY BINA AGARWAL

BEYOND FAMILY FARMING:
GENDERING THE COLLECTIVE

I am greatly honoured to be asked to deliver the Tenth Annual Balzan Lecture, and to such a distinguished audience, including Dr. Teresa Bellanova, Professor Enrico Decleva, Professor Quadrio-Curzio, Professor Marco Fortis, and the many members of the Accademia de Lincei, the Universities in Rome, and international organisations. I am also very glad to see so many students here today, and look forward to a lively interaction following my presentation.

INTRODUCTION

In 2016 the United Nations launched the Sustainable Development Goals as a "universal call to action, to end poverty, protect the planet, and ensure that all people enjoy peace and prosperity". Food security, sustainable livelihoods and social inclusion are key elements of the Goals. Yet, surprisingly, little attention has been paid to the institutions needed to deliver these Goals.

In this lecture I will argue that the institutional transformation of agriculture is essential for increasing farm productivity, improving farmer welfare, and enhancing gender equality. In particular, we need a model of farming that transcends the small family farms that dominate agriculture globally. This is an issue on which I have been researching for several years, and which I have been able to extend further using my Balzan Prize research funds. I will share today some aspects of my findings.[1]

---

[1] For this lecture, I have drawn especially on four of my papers, AGARWAL (2010, 2018, 2019, forthcoming).

Numerically, family farms constitute 88% of the world's 570 million farms (FAO 2014; GRAEUB et al. 2016). If we match this with the statistic that 84% of all farms across 111 countries are under 2 hectares in size (FAO 2014), we can surmise that most family farmers are also smallholders. Small family farmers, however, are facing a crisis in many developing countries. They have serious resource constraints, dwindling plot sizes, and fragmented holdings. This is playing out against a backdrop of climate change, limited non-farm jobs, and a feminisation of agriculture.

For example, in 2012, 43% of all farm workers in Asia and 47% in Africa were female, with percentages close to 50 in many Southeast Asian and East Asian countries. And these percentages have been growing, since typically more men than women move to non-farm jobs, leaving women to manage the family farms. This is what I mean by the process of feminisation of agriculture. It is a global phenomenon. The one exception is Europe where we see the masculinisation of farming, with more men than women continuing as farmers. Elsewhere, and especially in developing countries, however, both household food security and a country's agricultural growth are likely to depend increasingly on the performance of women farmers.

Women farmers, however, are even more resource constrained than small male farmers. Take land, the most important productive resources in rural areas. Although rather few countries collect gender-disaggregated macro-data on land ownership, existing figures are illustrative and show high gender inequality. In Asia, in the four countries (not including India) for which we have nationally representative figures, only 14 to 37% of landowners are found to be women (KIERAN et al. 2015). In India, in my own recent analysis, I found that only 14% of landowners across nine major states were women, and they owned only 11% of agricultural land (AGARWAL, ANTHWAL and MAHESH 2020). This included jointly owned land. In Africa, the average figures across ten countries show that only 22% of landowners are women, including joint owners (Doss et al. 2015). In Latin America the figures are 11 to 27% across several countries (DEERE and LEON 2003). Most studies do not examine the quality of land owned by gender, but an ongoing study for Malawi found that plots women owned were of poorer quality than those owned by men, which reduced the productivity of women's plots (KILIC and GOURLEY 2020).

These gender gaps reflect male bias in inheritance laws, government land distribution policies, and social norms. Women also face gender bias in access to irrigation, credit, technology, and other essentials. And they have limited bargaining power with the state and markets. As a result, most studies in Africa and Asia find that family farms managed by women have lower productivity than those managed by men (FAO 2010). At the same time, within male-managed family farms, women typically remain unpaid workers, lacking both autonomy in decision-making and independent identities as farmers (AGARWAL 2020). We thus need to explore farming models beyond family farms and beyond individually managed female farms.

Could a solution lie in group farming, involving resource pooling and joint cultivation? Could this model help women farmers overcome their resource constraints and enhance their productivity and profits? Can it also enhance their capabilities and empower them socially and politically? Before answering these questions, consider what group farming involves and its history.

HISTORY OF GROUP FARMING

Cooperation in farming can range from single purpose to multipurpose to fully integrated. Globally, single purpose marketing cooperatives are common, especially in the dairy industry. There has been a long tradition of this in Europe (ALMAS 2010). In developing countries, India's Amul milk cooperative with several million members is an important example. In between we find medium to multipurpose cooperation, such as for buying machines and crop planning. But none of these involve cooperation in production. Group farming goes much beyond these forms of cooperation. It involves resource pooling and intense cooperation on a daily basis for collective production, needing complex coordination.

The idea of farming collectively is not new. In fact, there have been at least four previous waves of collective farming. The first wave is the most famous (or *infamous*) and linked to socialism. Socialist collectives were formed through forced collectivization of peasant farms in the USSR, Eastern Europe and China, as well as other countries. These had seriously adverse effects on farm output and farmer welfare, especially in the USSR, and in varying degree in Europe, China and elsewhere, depending on how soon they relaxed the most stringent provisions (AGARWAL 2010). The second wave came in the 1960s when farmer cooperatives involving joint production were promoted, mostly top-down, in the post-colonial countries of Asia, Africa and Latin America, as part of agrarian reform. These efforts also largely failed or had mixed effects. The third wave, again going back to the 1960s, relates to group farming initiatives in Europe, especially France (AGARWAL and DORIN 2019). Formed voluntarily, these group farms were successful and have grown in number, but remain largely male-managed. And the fourth wave came in the 1990s when group farms emerged in many post-socialist countries such as Romania, Kyrgyzstan, East Germany and Nicaragua. Here farming families pooled resources to overcome land and machine scarcity. They were more productive and profitable than individual family farms, but were again mostly male-managed (see e.g. SABATES-WHEELER 2002, MATHIJS, and SWINNEN 2001, and the collation of evidence across regions in AGARWAL 2010).

In fact, *all* earlier collective ventures (socialist and non-socialist) were highly gender unequal. In the USSR, women in collective farms were concentrated in manual jobs that were designated less skilled and carried lower pay. For instance, only 0.8% of tractor drivers and 1.4% of machine handlers were female, and 85% of women employees compared to 66% of male workers were in jobs labelled 'unskilled'. In socialist China and Vietnam, again, women earned less work points than men, even when doing the harder tasks. Collectivities formed in non-socialist regimes, with the family as the production unit, were subject to another kind of gender bias, namely that embedded in the longstanding gender division of labour. Even in France, until 2010, spouses could not form group farms, until intensive lobbying by many women farmers led to change (AGARWAL and DORIN 2019).

However, the fifth wave of farm collectives, which occurred in India, is based on a very different model from all previous cases (AGARWAL forthcoming). In the 2000s, two states of India undertook experiments in all-women group farms. Under these initiatives – in Kerala and Telangana – rural women (and only women) were encouraged to lease in land collectively, pool their labour and capital, and cultivate jointly. They were voluntarily constituted, egalitarian, and managed entirely by women. Importantly, they were a collective of individuals, not a collective of family farms. And they recognized women as farmers in their individual capacity, outside the domain of family farms. Women could also exercise autonomy in farm decision-making. But how productive and profitable were they? To test this, I undertook primary surveys in both states during 2012-14, for a sample of group farms and individual family farmers (95% of which were male managed).

CONCEPTUAL ISSUES

Conceptually, we would expect resource pooling and joint cultivation to bring economic benefits to small farmers in general. For instance, group farming could help enlarge farm size through pooling owned or leased land. This would improve economic viability and help farmers reap economies of scale. Assessments for all-India by two American economists show that an increase in farm size starting from much below 2 hectares and going up to 8 hectares, significantly increases per hectare profits (FOSTER and ROSENZWEIG 2011).

Also, groups can bring other advantages, such as:
– they help save on hired labour
– they bring in a larger pool of funds and inputs
– they can tap into a greater diversity of skills than found in one person or family
– they enable farmers to take risks and experiment with risk-prone higher value crops with larger payoffs
– they help spread losses among a greater number
– they improve the farmers' ability to deliver on contracts
– and they raise farmers' bargaining power in markets and with governments.

For women farmers, these gains are likely to be even greater than for men, since women face greater economic constraints. Also, working in a group can help women overcome the social restrictions on the public interactions that they face in many cultures.

Group farms can be constituted by leasing in land, or pooling the members' own land, or a mix of both. But since rather few women own land, they may have few alternatives to taking up the land-lease model with its attendant constraints. Economic empowerment could, in turn, lead to social and political empowerment. But first consider the economic effects.

Genesis and Structure

The basic model of group farms taken up in Kerala and Telangana was of women leasing land, pooling labour and capital, and sharing costs and benefits. If the leased land belonged to a group member, the rent was settled in advance, and the member was expected to contribute the same labour and share the same input costs as other members. The women could also work on their family farms alongside. Task rotation allowed them enough flexibility to do so, or even take up wage work in some seasons.

In Kerala, the initial idea of group farming came from village women who had experimented with leasing land jointly. But the larger programme was crafted by senior government officials and intellectuals (see AGARWAL forthcoming). It was structured around the Self-Help Group (SHG) model which, in turn, evolved from micro-credit models. In Kerala this was further modified to constitute village-level neighbourhood groups (NHGs). These neighbourhood groups undertake savings-cum-credit, and some group members can then start group enterprises, including group farming. The whole programme is located in a multi-level structure of governance with three pillars. The first pillar is the Government's Poverty Eradication Mission (K. Mission). The second pillar is the Kudumbashree community network, constituted of Community Development Societies at the village council level. These are autonomous registered bodies with elected office bearers, with NHGs as the bottom tier. These Societies mediate on behalf of the women's groups with the government on the one hand and with the village council, which is the third pillar, on the other hand.

The group farms are constituted of women who are prior members of the NHGs. While not all NHG members take up group farming (hence there is some self-selection), on important variables such as schooling, economic status, and credit access there is little systematic difference between NHG women who take up group farming and those who do not. The groups can access subsidised credit through the central government's agricultural development Bank, NABARD. They also receive state government support, including a startup grant, technical information, training from experts, and crop-specific incentives. This support somewhat levels the playing field for women relative to men, but not fully, since some gender-based disadvantages persist (as discussed further below). Today, there are over 64,000 such farms across Kerala, involving over 300,000 women.

In Telangana – the second state I studied – group farming was launched in 2001 by the United Nations Development Programme and government of India, within a five-year support framework. It was implemented through APMSS (the Andhra Pradesh Mahila Samatha Society), a quasi-NGO set up in 1993 to promote women's empowerment through education. APMSS set up sanghas or women's collectives (one per village), federated at the district level. These pre-existing collectives took up group farming in 500 villages. Typically, all sangha members in the project villages joined; hence there was little self-selection. Each group received a small grant, implements, training and other support, but much less than in Kerala. Also, government support ended once UNDP funding ceased in 2005. Yet, encouragingly, I found that 50% of the 500 groups had continued to farm, overseen by APMSS, when I began my research.

I compared group farms in each state with small family farms of 2 hectares or less in the same state, to assess if group farms were more productive and profitable than small family farms, as we may expect conceptually.

In Kerala, the districts selected were Alappuzha, which is dominated by rice cultivation, and Thrissur, where commercial cultivation of banana is common. Both districts also grow vegetables. My Kerala sample consisted of 250 farms (69 all-women groups and 181 individual family farms owning 2 hectares or less). In Telangana, the sample consisted of 763 farms, of which 70 were all-women group farms, and 693 individual farms, again owning 2 hectares or less and located in three semi-arid districts (see AGARWAL 2018 for details). Weekly data were collected in 2012-13 and data gaps were filled in 2013-14 from both states, for every input and output, for each crop and plot in the sample farms. This was a huge data collection exercise, which proved to be incredibly complicated and difficult in terms of coordination, information gathering and cross-checking. Most studies use one time or one season memory recall for collecting such data. But memory recall, especially on labour used, does not provide accurate information; hence I decided to collect the data every week. In addition, information on farm and farmer characteristics, difficulties faced, perceptions of benefits, etc. was collected via focus group discussions, from both group farms and individual family farms.

Characteristics of the Groups

Kerala's and Telangana's groups differ in size and social composition. Kerala's group farms had an average of 6 members. Almost all the women were literate, two-thirds had completed secondary school or above; and only 9% were 60 years of age or more. Most importantly, the groups were heterogeneous across caste and religious lines (80% were Hindus) and included both poor and less poor homes. This heterogeneity goes against the common assumption in most collective action theory in economics that homogeneity is necessary for effective cooperation.

Heterogeneity was consciously promoted under this programme for at least two reasons: it represented their neighbourhoods, which were themselves heterogeneous, and it was expected to ensure leadership. The K. Mission's logic was that local women's leadership does not come from the poorest but from those just above poverty line. In addition, I found during my fieldwork that heterogeneity provided a wider base of social capital for accessing land. Potential social divides were overcome by rotating weekly meetings across households of diverse castes and classes. In contrast, Telangana's groups were larger, with an average of 22 members (some even had 54 members). Most were low caste Hindus; 38% were illiterate; and 17% were 60 years of age or older. In both states almost all women members came from small landowning farming families.

The sampled group farms were larger in land size than individual farms, so they had some advantage of size. In Kerala, the average group farm was almost 1 hectare while the average individual farm was 0.35 hectares. In Telangana, the group farms were 2 hectares on average, while the individual farms were on average 1 hectare in size. All the groups leased in land, mostly from outside the group on a cash rent basis. Individual farmers, by contrast, owned all or most of the land they cultivated.

Despite the support of the state noted above, women's groups still faced four initial disadvantages relative to the largely male-run family farms. First, their dependence on leased inland involved high transaction costs in finding suitable land in a single plot, and created insecurity of tenure since leases were oral and informal. Land access was in fact the biggest hurdle, especially in Telangana. Here the group farms, constituted mainly of scheduled castes, had limited access to the land of the well-endowed upper castes. For illustration, consider this citation from women in Medak district:

> The landlords in the village think that since all our members belong to the scheduled caste community, if they lease to us we will get the land title in the group's name. So none is prepared to lease land to us.

Second, oral leases meant women lacked proof of being farmers and so were unable to easily access government subsidies. Third, women continued to face structural biases in access to inputs, extension services, machines and markets and often failed to get inputs in time. Fourth, rather few women had prior experience in managing farms. Most had been workers on family farms managed by male members or housewives. This meant they had to gain experience on many aspects of farm management.

Some, but not all, of these disadvantages were overcome with state support and forming groups. And they dealt with collective action problems, such as someone not turning up for work, by insisting that the absentee replace her labour with the labour of another family member or hired a labourer, or paid a fine. Despite these challenges, how well did the women's collectives perform vis-a-vis the largely male-managed individual family farms? In Kerala they did strikingly well in most part, but in Telangana less so.

PRODUCTION AND PROFIT

(a) Productivity

I found that in Kerala, taking both districts together, group farms relative to individual family farms had 1.8 times the average annual output per hectare. Also in the major commercial crop, banana, group farms had 1.6 times the average yields of individual farms. Only in paddy did women's groups do less well. These results are supported by my regression analysis which controlled for input use, labour and other factors. The regressions showed that a shift from individual farms to women's group farms was associated with an increase in annual output by 30%. In banana, a shift from individual to group farms was linked with an increase in output by 348% (see AGARWAL 2018 for details).

The banana story was notable. Although all farmers try and fine-tune their harvest and sale of bananas to take advantage of high prices during the festival season, the women's groups were able to work the market especially well. Some had negotiated contracts with local temples to supply special banana varieties. As groups they could ensure delivery better than small individual farmers. In both annual output and banana yields, the most important input driving the output was labour, followed by land. In paddy, however, the groups performed less well than individual farmers largely due to their inability to lease in good quality paddy land, which landowners self-cultivated and did not lease out.

In Telangana, however, group farms performed worse than individual farms in their annual value of output per hectare for all crops, and for food grains alone. But they performed almost as well as individual farms in cotton. The crop-specific regressions bore this out. For food grains, individual farms had significantly higher yields than group farms, but there was no notable difference between farm types in cotton yields. This suggests that women's groups could have done better with cotton. The NGO promoting these groups strongly encouraged them to grow food grains and not the region's commercial crop, cotton, arguing that food grains would increase their food security. This emphasis on growing food grains for food security is a common assumption in civil society. This may well be a good assumption in certain contexts, but in the semi-arid zones of Telangana with limited irrigation, the concentration on food grains left the women's groups vulnerable to low output.

(b) Profitability

Now consider net returns. These were calculated by deducting all paid out costs from the total value of output, but without imputing values to owned land or family labour.

In Kerala, 82-84% of both group and individual farms got positive net returns. But for group farms, the average net returns per farm were strikingly higher than for individual farms, and these differences were statistically significant, after controlling for district-level effects in the regressions. In fact, the mean net return per farm of Rs. 121,048 for groups was five times higher than that of small individual farms, and three times that year's state average of Rs. 45,000 per farm for the same year. Moreover, per hectare returns were 1.6 times higher in the group farms. The results demonstrate that despite difficulties in leasing land, women's group farms can notably outperform individual male farmers in small-scale commercial farming. Indeed, even in Telangana, group farms made up for low productivity in annual net returns, since they spent less on hired labour.

COMPARING THE TWO STATES

Overall, why did Kerala do so well and did Telangana not? Three types of factors are likely to underlie this divergent performance of the two states. First, Kerala had consistent government support, including technical training and incentives. This was limited in Telangana and ended after five years, when United Nations Development Programme support ended. Moreover, Kerala's groups took advantage of the government's subsidized credit scheme for groups via The National Bank for Agriculture and Rural Development, but Telangana's groups did not.

Second, Kerala's innovative three pillar institutional structure played a key role. In particular, the autonomous Community Development Societies could negotiate effectively on behalf of group farms with the state government's Kudumbashree Mission for various types of technical and other help. Telangana's groups depended on federations with little direct negotiating power with the state government.

Third, Kerala's group members were heterogeneous, educated, and relatively young, and had wide social networks. Telangana's groups were largely composed of scheduled caste, relatively poor women with a limited social base, and many were also illiterate. Moreover, Kerala's groups had six members on average, enabling high per capita returns and easier coordination. Telangana's groups had 22 members on average (and some had over 50 members). This greatly reduced per capita returns and made coordination of labour time much more difficult.

Fourth, Kerala gained by choosing more commercial crops, they had better land access due to their wider social network, and a favourable local ecology with high rainfall and irrigation. In contrast, Telangana lost by an over-emphasis on food grains under semi-arid climatic conditions with poorly developed irrigation.

Fifth, how the initiatives were conceptualised made a difference. Kerala focused on livelihood enhancement and interlinked social empowerment. Telangana introduced group farming onto a pre-existing programme for social empowerment.

Nevertheless, in both states, group farming, catalysed by external interventions, provided women farmers an important alternative to being unpaid workers on family farms.

CAPABILITY ENHANCEMENT

Beyond production, qualitative evidence indicates that group farming has enhanced women's capabilities, and transformed their lives. First, women have developed stronger identities as farmers in their own right, rather than being seen simply as labourers or farm wives.

> Group farming has enriched my farming experience. Through the group, I realized that I have good leadership qualities and could also manage the technical aspects of farming. Other group members now listen to me carefully. (Women's group farm, Kerala)

Second, group farming has familiarized women with a wide range of public institutions and services.

> Before joining the group [...], we had no contacts with bank officials, agricultural officers and government officials. After registering as a group, we could start a bank account, attend [training] classes, and develop a good rapport with bank officers, ward members and Krishi Bhawan [agricultural department] officers. (Women's group farm, Kerala)

Third, group members have learnt to negotiate in multiple markets. In land markets they judge land quality and negotiate lease terms; in input markets they assess prices; and in Telangana, many have learnt to successfully negotiate access to storage for their crops in market centres:

> Earlier women were never seen in the market yards. Now they are very visible, bringing their produce, negotiating with buyers, and, if necessary, negotiating for physical space in the market yard to keep their produce till they decide to sell it. (P. Prashanthi, Director APMSS)

Most importantly, women have learnt to make production decisions and manage the farms independently.

In addition, women report being much more respected within families and communities. Consider what they said:

> Earlier, villagers were disrespectful to us and would call us by our nicknames. Also if we went to see an upper-caste villager we were made to sit on the floor. But now conditions have changed. As group members we are farming on our own, and can also enlighten villagers by conducting social awareness programmes…. So now villagers respect us and call us by our own names (SC women's group in Telangana).

> I was just a housewife before joining the group farm. Everybody used to call me by my husband's name. Nobody knew me by my own name. Now the situation has changed. (Women's group farm, Kerala)

In Kerala, in most cases, women say they control the income they earn from the group farms.

Also, in both states, group farm members have been standing for village council elections and many have been winning. They can thus provide an important bridge between the village councils and the group farms.

BROADER REFLECTIONS

Through these detailed examples of women farmers' collectives cooperating for sustainable livelihoods, I have sought to demonstrate that institutional innovations can lead to important economic and social gains. In agriculture, they can reduce the effects of state failure and market failure for the disadvantaged. Even though the groups cannot overcome some deeply embedded inequalities such as in land ownership, they provide a means of accessing land and other inputs which those cultivating individually, especially women, often cannot access. The groups also provide recognition and autonomy to women farmers in ways that family farming rarely does.

For creating successful and sustainable groups, however, the divergence between Kerala and Telangana offers lessons on what should be done and what should be avoided. Kerala provides most of the lessons on the former and Telangana on the latter. But overall, we can affirm that in both states group farming can level the playing field for women to a considerable degree and empower them as farmers. From such empirical examples, we can also refine collective action theory beyond governing common property resources, to take account of the specificities of private property.

Let us now consider a question which must be in the minds of many of you: for success do the groups necessarily have to be constituted only of women? The answer is complex and depends on context. Many grassroots activists argue that all-women groups cooperate better and are less prone to conflicts. And when conflicts do occur, they get resolved and do not escalate in the way that conflicts in men's groups tend to do. This is because women, especially village women, are more dependent on one another on a daily basis due to resource scarcity. Groups also help women overcome restrictive social norms.

For instance, I found in my research on community forest management in India and Nepal that women were more likely to participate in decision-making within forest protection groups when they were a critical mass of 25-33%. And all-women groups protecting forests in Nepal had significantly better conservation outcomes than mixed gender groups with few women or all-male groups. Similarly, when self-help groups (SHGs) began in India and micro-credit Grameen Bank groups began in Bangladesh, there were both male and female groups. Over time, however, 90% of the groups that have survived are all-female groups with excellent repayment records. Some activists also argue that being in all-women groups helps women gain self-confidence to be able to work better in mixed-gender groups. At the same time, political power and economic resources are largely concentrated with men. Hence dependence solely on all-women's groups could prove restrictive. We thus need to be open to both gender-balanced mixed groups and all-women's groups.

That an openness to groups of varying gender composition can bear fruit is also borne out by the recent emergence of group farming in eastern India and Nepal. Constituted by a consortium of local and international research institutes, and led by the International Water Management Institute in Nepal, some 20 farmers' collectives were formed in 2015 in six villages, two each in Nepal, Bihar and North Bengal. The collectives, each formed by 4 to 10 marginal and tenant farmers, have evolved into four different models with varying gender composition and levels of cooperation (SUDGEN *et al.* forthcoming). Five of the groups are all-women, two are all-male and the rest are mixed gender (with the percentages of women ranging from 12.5 to 87.5). Some of the groups work collectively for the full year, others do so for one season. Some lease in most of their land, others have consolidated their own small plots. Over the past five years, all the groups have recorded economic gains. For example, by jointly cultivating larger contiguous plots they have increased their efficiency of labour and machine use for land preparation and irrigation, reaped economies in input purchase, and raised farm yields, which are much higher now than those recorded on their individual farms before they formed the collectives. In addition, some of the groups have been able to challenge old feudal relations with landlords by refusing to provide free labour, and bargain down the rents they have to pay for leasing in land.

Let me now end with a brief focus on a concept deriving from groups and cooperation that has caught the international imagination. This is the concept of the social and solidarity economy. Although the concept is still evolving, there is agreement that it covers various forms of citizens' associations (social movements, self-help groups, etc.) which cooperate for production and exchange in inclusive ways, and interact with the state and markets on behalf of citizens. A key question that remains unanswered, however, is: what motivates people to cooperate? Is it just enlightened self-interest or is there also some sense of solidarity beyond self-interest?

I believe it helps to distinguish between what I term strategic solidarity and empathetic solidarity. The women group farmers I have been researching were motivated by both. They began with strategic solidarity, undertaking group farming for economic viability. But, over time, empathetic solidarity also emerged: women now help each other in times of personal need, including illness, and in Telangana, the groups show particular empathy towards elderly women who are treated as equal members, on the grounds that they provide useful experiential knowledge, even though they cannot contribute much labour. Hence while collectives may initially be built on enlightened self-interest for strategic benefits, over time there is much scope for moving from self-interest to other-regarding interest, and from individual to collective responsibility. And this is not specifically a female trait. Even Adam Smith, who argued so eloquently for free competition and market exchange, recognised this as a universal trait in his *Theory of Moral Sentiments*, when he wrote (SMITH 1759 [1966]):

> How selfish soever man may be supposed, there are evidently some principles in his nature which interest him in the fortune of others, and render their happiness necessary to him, though he derives nothing from it, except the pleasure of seeing it.

Indeed, as many group farmers (both women and men) argue, cooperation is often worth it simply because you enjoy working together. In a world of growing individualism, it is an important reminder that not everything needs to have instrumental worth.

SELECTED REFERENCES

AGARWAL, B. (2010). "Rethinking Agricultural Production Collectivities." *Economic and Political Weekly* 55(9): 64-78.

AGARWAL, B. (2018). "Can Group Farms Outperform Individual Family Farms? Empirical Insights from India." *World Development* 108: 57-73.

AGARWAL, B. (2019). "Does Group Farming Empower Rural Women? Lessons from India's Experiments." *Journal of Peasant Studies* (July) https://www.tandfonline.com/doi/full/10.1080/03066150.2019.1628020.

AGARWAL, B. (2020). "Labouring for Livelihoods: Gender, Productivity and Collectivity." *Indian Journal of Labour Economics* 63(1): 21-37.

AGARWAL, B. (forthcoming). "A Tale of Two Experiments: Institutional Innovations in Women's Group Farming." *Canadian Journal of Development Studies*.

AGARWAL, B. and B. DORIN (2019). "Group Farming in France: Why do Some Regions Have More Cooperative Ventures than Others?" *Environment and Planning A: Economy and Space* 51(3): 781-804.

AGARWAL, B., P. ANTHWAL, and M. MAHESH (2020). "Which Women Own Land in India? Between Divergent Data Sets, Measures and Laws." GDI Working paper 2020-043. Global Development Institute, The University of Manchester.

ALMAS, R. (2010) "I Have Seen the Future and It Works: How Joint I May Solve Contradictions between Technological Level and Farm Structure in Norwegian Dairy Production." In: BONANNO, A.B., R. JUSSAUMA, Y. KAWAMURA, M. SHUCKSMITH, (eds). *From Community to Consumption: New and Classical Themes in Rural Sociological Research*. Bingley: Emerald Group Publishing Limited, pp. 3-16.

DEERE, C.D and M. LEON (2003). "The Gender Asset Gap: Land in Latin America." *World Development* 31: 925-947.

DOSS, C., C. KOVARIK, A. PETERMAN, A. QUISUMBING, and M.V. BOLD (2015). "Gender Inequalities in Ownership and Control of Land in Africa: Myth and Reality." *Agricultural Economics* 46: 403-434.

FAO. (2011). *The State of Food and Agriculture Report. Women in Agriculture*. Rome: UN Food and Agricultural Organisation.

FAO (2014). *The State of Food and Agriculture Report. Innovation in Family Farming*. Rome: UN Food and Agricultural Organisation.

FOSTER, A. D., and M. ROSENZWEIG (2011). *Are Indian Farms too Small?* Mimeo, Providence: Brown University.

GRAEUB, B.E., CHAPPELL, M.J., WITTMAN, H., LEDERMANN, S., KERR, R.B., and GEMMILL-HERREN, B. (2016). "The State of Family Farms in the World." *World Development*, 87: 1-15.

KIERAN, C., SPROULE, K., DOSS, C., QUISUMBING, A., and KIM, S.M. (2015). "Examining Gender Inequalities in Land Rights Indicators in Asia." *Agricultural Economics*, 46 supplement 119-138.

KILIC, T. and GOURLEY, S. (2020). "Explaining the Gender Gap in Agricultural Productivity in Malawi: The Role of Soil Quality." Mimeo, Development Data Group, The World Bank, Washington DC.

MATHIJS, E. and J.F.M. SWINNEN (2001). "Production Organisation and Efficiency during Transition: An Empirical Analysis of East German Agriculture." *The Review of Economics and Statistics*, 83(1): 100-107.

SABATES-WHEELER R. (2002). "Farm Strategy, Self-Selection and Productivity: Can Small Farming Groups Offer Production Benefits in Post-Socialist Romania?" *World Development*, 30 (10): 1737-1753.

SMITH, A. (1759 [1966]). The *Theory of Moral Sentiments*, vol. 1. Reproductions of economic classics. New York: Augustus M. Kelly.

SUDGEN, F., AGARWAL, B., LEDER, S., SAIKIA, P., RAUT, M., KUMAR, A., and RAY, D. (forthcoming). "Experiments in Farmer Collectives in Eastern India and Nepal: Process, Benefits and Challenges." *Journal of Agrarian Change*.

COMMENTS AND DISCUSSION

Alberto Quadrio-Curzio (Moderator): After this outstanding Annual Balzan Lecture by Bina Agarwal, I have the pleasure to ask one member of our audience in particular, the Honourable Teresa Bellanova, Minister of Agriculture of the Italian Government, to take the floor and comment on the crucial issues of women in agriculture and women in the labour force in general. I might also add that Minister Bellanova's personal life and work is an outstanding example of the mission to give women in any field of work more freedom and opportunities.

Please, Minister Bellanova, the floor is yours.

Teresa Bellanova: I would like to offer some thoughts on the theme of agricultural work and women who work in the sector. From my early experience in the labour unions combatting illegal hiring in the agricultural sector, to my present engagement in Italian politics, I have been particularly concerned with social injustice as regards women workers. Agarwal's studies are fundamental for two reasons: first of all, in order to understand the dynamics of agricultural labour, especially in relation to the dimension of gender; and secondly to identify solutions that promote economic growth without increasing inequalities (or possibly reducing them) and without having a negative impact on the environment. I could refer to many figures that confirm the continued exploitation of the female workforce all over the world – all of which come back to Agarwal's research. We must boost women's productivity, especially if we intend to reach important objectives like Zero Hunger in 2030. Agarwal's work is revolutionary in its advocacy of a different way of doing agriculture in developing countries aimed at producing better living conditions, more equality, less environmental impact, and greater social justice. Agarwal's findings can be compared with the situation of agricultural labourers in Italy, where there is still much to be done to fight the continued exploitation of workers and their rights, not to mention discrimination against women in all sectors in Italy. I can end on a positive note, namely the recent measures taken by the Italian government to enable women to reconcile their professional lives with raising a family, like free nursery schools, or to help women agricultural entrepreneurs through financial bonuses including zero interest mortgages. In the end, Agarwal could become a reference point for Italy by stimulating reflection on more equitable and sustainable ways of farming from the human and environmental point of view, providing new ideas in terms of the organization of work and the size and governance of farms, and supporting decision-makers in adopting more just and effective measures that encourage growth and greater social justice.

Alberto Quadrio-Curzio: Thank you very much, Minister Bellanova, for your highly important comments that have bestowed a significant institutional endorsement on our evening. I am sure that Professor Agarwal will maintain your analysis for her future work which, as you have done, Minister, gives much hope to women agricultural workers for a better life.

Now we have some time for discussion, so whoever would like to express their thoughts or ask questions, Professor Agarwal is here, ready to respond.

FAO Representative: Good evening. My name is Olivier Cossée, from the Food and Agriculture Organization of the United Nations. I have written about and studied the feminisation of agriculture quite a lot. I would like to ask you a question about those female farmers. One of my intuitions is that if there is feminisation of agriculture, as there is in a number of countries, there might also be a need for the feminisation of support to agriculture. By that I mean support in veterinary services, extension services, and in mechanisation. For instance, the picture you showed of women tilling – the machine might be better adapted to female farmers if it was a bit lighter. So my question is: in your discussions with them, did you find that the support system needs to be adapted better to female farmers?

Bina Agarwal: Thank you very much. I am very happy that somebody from the FAO has come, given FAO's longstanding interest in women farmers. You are absolutely right about the need to adapt technology. In fact, in the Telangana case, during the project period there was a discussion with the women farmers about ways of developing lighter tools which would be more efficient and easier for women to handle. These were developed and tested with them. Moreover, in Africa – as you probably know – it has been found that if new technology is tested in women farmers' fields, it helps greatly in their adopting that technology. Typically, however, the male extension agents tend to go to male farmers' fields and rarely to women farmers' fields. Here having women extension agents with a special mandate to attend to women farmers can help. I remember there was considerable discussion about this in India in the late 1980s and early 1990s, but since then we have regressed and forgotten about it. We need to bring attention back to this issue, although today's generation of women farmers are perhaps less hesitant in communicating with male extension workers. Moreover, if women are working in a group, they are more able to overcome social barriers. I therefore agree with you that we need a feminisation of support services, but perhaps this need is less acute in terms of communicating information on new technologies than it was twenty years ago, although it still exists in terms of adapting machine designs.

As a footnote, I want to mention that a year ago I completed a survey on group farms in France, in the provinces of Ain and Saône-et-Loire. I am now analysing the data. I remember that one of the women farmers whom we interviewed showed us the large machines on her farm, and told us that the machines were too large for her to handle on her own. She therefore had to ask her brother or her father to help operate them. I am sure the Minister will have similar examples from Italy.

Giulia Zacchia: My name is Giulia Zacchia, of the Università "La Sapienza" in Rome, and infinite thanks for your talk. The seminar was truly touching, and the speech was concrete – just what was needed. This is a provocation. As regards the collection of data on Kerala, technical training was mentioned, that is, training courses. I wonder if the university might not also play a role in this game, and would thus raise the possibility of inserting this "third mission", this social impact that the university can have in a concrete way on society, and how it can work? And here is where the provocation comes into play. We have spoken of a social solidarity economy, could there also be a social solidarity knowledge that could be integrated in this through the role of the universities?

Bina Agarwal: Thank you. I can take more than one question at a time.

Sapienza post-doc: I am a post-doc at the Sapienza, as is Giulia. Thank you so much for your inspiring lecture. I have two questions. The first one is in some ways related to the first question. At the beginning of your lecture, you said that the agricultural sector in Europe is moving towards masculinisation. I would like to know the potential causes. My second question is why Kerala was successful while Telangana was not as successful. Do gender norms differ between these two regions? Are they a driving force explaining the different degrees of success?

Bina Agarwal: Thank you very much for those comments and questions. I think universities have a big role to play in supporting farmers. In fact, in my examples as well, in the case of Kerala, the government drew in agricultural universities to train the women farmers. Also, in the three-pillared organisational structure I mentioned in my lecture, the community networks of *Kudumbasree* are supported by government officers from the agricultural ministry as well as university faculties. Some of the experts have also been seconded to work on this programme. And most of them love this work, so even when they have to return to their institutions at the end of their tenure, they often try to come back to the programme. They see their work as socially relevant. I might also mention that in 2012, I travelled with a group of agroecologists and agricultural university teachers in the state of Minas Gerais in Brazil. We visited a number of farms where they were playing a very important role in helping farmers solve the problems they face in the field.

On your question about social solidarity and knowledge sharing, yes that is also important. In the case of Kerala, for example, some women were trained as Master Farmers to help other women farmers within their community. I feel it is important that we do not depend entirely on the government but also train village women in technical matters and extension. They, in turn, can support the community. In my fieldwork in India, I found it very interesting that many of the women said they felt empowered, since now even the male farmers in their village asked them for advice about technical matters, and what they should be doing on their farms. For these women, this was a new experience, since typically they were not seen as repositories of technical knowledge.

The question about masculinisation of agriculture in Europe is an interesting one and worth exploring further. Data on Europe needs to be disaggregated further, because I suspect we will find differences between southern Europe and northern Europe, and similarly within countries, such as between southern Italy and northern Italy. I think explaining why we see these patterns in Europe is a very good topic for a post-doc to take up. I don't have definitive answers on why you might see these regional differences, but it could be due to a mix of factors: cultural practices, migration patterns, crops grown, and government policies. In France, during my fieldwork, I found that on many group farms, the wives of farmers were doing the financial accounting work. They had the technical skills which their husbands did not always possess. It was interesting to see this, since typically it is incorrectly assumed that women are not very good at maths and science. But here they were the ones with those very skills. On your question about social norms, Kerala and Telangana do not differ greatly in this regard. Both states are in south India and they don't face the same constraints as women face in northern India. It is true that some of the communities in Kerala are matrilineal and there is almost 100% female literacy in the state, which is not the case in Telangana. But the main reasons for the differential performance of group farms in Kerala and Telangana lie, in my view, in the other factors I talked about, namely the governance structures, group composition, local ecology, and government support.

Alberto Quadrio-Curzio: The final question is from Professor Brunori, who has been the President of the Class of Natural, Mathematical and Physical Sciences of the Lincei.

Maurizio Brunori: Thank you very much for your talk. Mine is not a technical question. I just want to extrapolate a single point from this very broad view of your work of many years. I was very impressed by one fact that you mentioned, that these groups were constituted of only women. Was this more productive in some way? Was it easier to handle in terms of social relationships? And this is going to be so simple that it could be inaccurate – is it because, in being together on all-women ground they may feel more secure that their dignity will be preserved, so to speak?

Bina Agarwal: I read two elements in your question. One is why all-women's groups are so successful, and the other is the effect of such groups on the non-economic aspects of empowerment, such as dignity and respect. On the first, I think one could make a general claim that people who are more interdependent are much more likely to cooperate than people who are not. And in contexts of scarcity, be it scarcity of knowledge or scarcity of resources, you will have much more to gain from cooperation than non-cooperation. In this sense, the fact that women are noted to work well together is likely to have much to do with their interdependence and relative lack of resources. But the second part of the question, which is on the non-economic gains from group formation, yes, I think forming groups does make a big difference.

There is an additional issue that your question raises: would simply forming a group make a difference, or forming a group for an *economic* purpose make a difference? On the basis of my research, I feel that bringing economic gains to the family and to the community makes an additional difference. Many examples of social movements show that if women come together in groups, they are better respected in communities, but if they come together for economic purposes and demonstrably show that they are productive and earn an independent income, this additionally enhances the respect they gain. And there are two elements to dignity: one lies in the community recognising a person's worth, the other lies in her family recognising her worth. The latter can also greatly improve intra-household gender dynamics. I was very struck by what one of the women said. She said that after they formed a group and she brought in earnings, her husband took her to the cinema for the first time since their marriage many years ago! To her, that was a big deal!

Thank you very much Alberto. I also warmly thank everybody for coming, and especially to Minister Teresa Bellanova I would like to say – thank you very much for your very kind remarks, and especially your remarks expressing solidarity with the cause of women farmers. I hope that there will be occasions where we might collaborate to take some of these ideas forward. Thanks again to everyone.

Alberto Quadrio-Curzio: Thank you very much, Bina, for your moving and thoughtful talk, from which I have learned quite a lot. Before closing this meeting, I have to add two words about an initiative in which I am trying to involve Bina. It has to do with women scientists in developing countries, and I hope to be able to do something regarding that next year. Before closing, I also have to say something in another capacity, as this is the tenth Annual Balzan Lecture. As you know, every year the Balzan Foundation does one Annual Balzan Lecture, which is given by one of the Prize winners. This is the tenth one. The first one started in 2010, but, as far as I know, this is the first one by an economist, a social scientist and an institutional scientist, and also by a person who has spent a good deal of her life to work for the common good, for human progress and gender equality, and all the significant aims of human development. Having said that, I once again extend my thanks to the Minister of Agriculture, to Professor Decleva, and to all the people here. One final word, Bina is a fellow of the Lincei of course, and she is wearing the lynx pin that shows this affiliation. I hope we will see Bina in Italy – especially here at the Lincei – again soon.

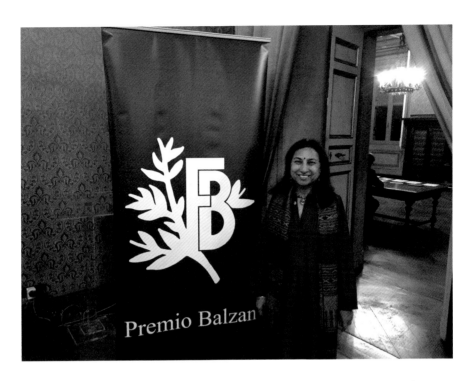

Bina Agarwal, 2017 Balzan Prize for Gender Studies, before delivering the 2019 Annual Balzan Lecture, *Beyond Family Farming: Gendering the Collective*.

The audience during the 2019 Annual Balzan Lecture.

Bina Agarwal and Alberto Quadrio-Curzio, Vice President of the Balzan Foundation "Prize", President Emeritus of the Accademia dei Lincei and President of the Joint Commission Balzan-Lincei-Swiss Academies.

Standing: Enrico Decleva, President of the Balzan Foundation "Prize"; at the table: Bina Agarwal and Alberto Quadrio-Curzio.

The audience at the 2019 Annual Balzan Lecture.

Italian Minister of Agriculture Teresa Bellanova comments on Bina Agarwal's 2019 Annual Balzan Lecture *Beyond Family Farming: Gendering the Collective*.

BINA AGARWAL

BIOGRAPHICAL AND BIBLIOGRAPHICAL DATA

Bina Agarwal, born in 1951, is an Indian citizen. She is Professor of Development Economics and Environment at the Global Development Institute, School for Environment, Education and Development, at the University of Manchester. A Fellow of the Indian Association for Agricultural Economics, she is also Member of the Accademia Nazionale dei Lincei, Rome, Italy, and Officer of the Order of Agricultural Merit of the Government of France.

After earning a BA (Hons) in Economics from the University of Delhi in 1970, she completed another BA in Economics (the Economics Tripos) from the University of Cambridge in 1972 and an MA from the University of Cambridge in 1977. In 1978 she completed her PhD from the Delhi School of Economics, University of Delhi.

Prior to joining the University of Manchester in 2012, she worked at the Institute of Economic Growth, Delhi University (where she continues to be affiliated) as Associate Professor of Economics (1981-1988), Professor of Economics (1988-2012), and Head of the Population Research Center (1996-98, 2002-04, 2009-12). From 1972 to 1974 she was Research Associate on the Planning Commission and Ford Foundation Growth Center Project for Regional Planning at the Council for Social Development, Delhi.

Bina Agarwal has held distinguished teaching and research positions at many universities, including Harvard, Princeton, Michigan, Minnesota, IDS (Sussex), and the New York University School of Law. She was Harvard's first Daniel Ingalls Visiting Professor and later a Research Fellow at the Ash Institute, Kennedy School of Government as well as a fellow of Radcliffe's Bunting Institute at Harvard.

She has been President of the International Society for Ecological Economics, Vice President of the International Economic Association, President of the International Association for Feminist Economics, Board Member of the Global Development Network, and one of the twenty-one members of the Commission for the Measurement of Economic Performance and Social Progress. She has served on the UN Committee for Development Policy (New York) and United Nations Research Institute for Social Development (Geneva), and holds honorary doctorates from the Institute of Social Studies in the Netherlands and the University of Antwerp in Belgium.

Bina Agarwal has authored over ninety academic papers and twenty general essays. A selection follows.

As author:

– *A Field of One's Own: Gender and Land Rights in South Asia.* Cambridge University Press, 1994. CUP South Asian edition 1995. Reprinted 1996, 1998.
– *Cold Hearths and Barren Slopes: The Woodfuel Crisis in the Third World, London.* Zed Books; Delhi: Allied Publishers; Maryland: Riverdale Publishers, 1986. Reprinted 1988.
– *Gender and Green Governance.* Oxford University Press, 2010; Indian edition 2010.
– *Gender Challenges. Vol. 1: Agriculture, Technology and Food Security; Vol. 2: Property, Family and the State; Vol. 3: Environmental Change and Collective Action. Mechanisation in Indian Agriculture.* [Delhi: Allied Publishers, 1983; reprinted 1986.] New Delhi: Oxford University Press, 2016.

As editor:

– *Capabilities, Freedom and Equality: Amartya Sen's Work from a Gender Perspective.* Delhi: Oxford University Press, 2006. Also published without Sen's original writings under the title *Amartya Sen's Work and Ideas: A Gender Perspective.* London: Routledge, 2005. Editors: Bina Agarwal, Jane Humphries, and Ingrid Robeyns.
– *Psychology, Rationality and Economic Behaviour: Challenging Standard Assumptions.* London: Palgrave, 2005; Indian edition 2008 Editors: Bina Agarwal, and Alessandro Vercelli.
– *Structures of Patriarchy: State, Community and Household in Modernising Asia.* London: Zed Books; Delhi: Kali for Women, 1988; reprinted in paperback 1990. Editor: Bina Agarwal.
– *Women and Work in the World Economy.* London: Macmillan Press, 1991. Editors: Nancy Folbre, Barbara Bergmann, Bina Agarwal and Maria Floro.
– *Women, Poverty and Ideology in Asia: Contradictory Pressures, Uneasy Resolutions.* London: Macmillan Press, 1989. Editors: Haleh Afshar and Bina Agarwal.

INSTITUTIONAL INNOVATIONS,
GENDER AND THE ECONOMY

Adviser for the Balzan General Prize Committee: Marjan Schwegman

As Professor of Development Economics and Environment at the Global Development Institute, School for Environment, Education and Development at the University of Manchester, UK and through her affiliation with the Institute of Economic Growth, Delhi, at which she was former Professor and Director, Bina Agarwal will draw on the logistical support of both institutions for taking her research forward.

Agarwal's Balzan Prize research funds will be used to pursue three research trajectories under the broad theme: "Institutional innovations, gender and the economy". Each trajectory, presented as an independent but interrelated project, will involve collaboration with young early-career scholars as well as mid-career and senior colleagues. The projects will also build research capacity among post-Masters and doctoral students by employing them as research analysts or co-partners. In addition, workshops will be organized to share project results with policymakers and civil society, so that the research can have an impact on and make a difference to people's lives. This would also be in keeping with the larger aims of the Balzan Prize of fostering human well-being.

Project 1. Group farming and collective action theory in Asia and Europe

This project focuses on an alternative model of farming based on small farmer cooperation, and aims to break new ground in institutional analysis and collective action theory. The context is an endemic and intensifying crisis of food security, played out against the backdrop of climate change and high inequalities in land distribution.

Most farming systems in developing countries today are characterized by millions of small family farms, typically facing severe constraints in access to inputs, credit, irrigation, resource conserving technology, and markets. As a result, their productivity remains far below potential and they are unable to achieve sustainable livelihoods. Can a model based on a group approach, involving the pooling of land, labour and capital by smallholders, provide an alternative? Can it help small farmers (an increasing percentage of whom are women) overcome their input constraints, enjoy scale economies, and enhance their bargaining power vis-a-vis markets and states? In particular, can such a model outperform individual family farms in terms of productivity and profits to ensure more secure livelihoods for those involved?

This is a relatively unexplored field, since most work on collective action has focused on the governance of common pool resources and not on cooperation around private property resources and farming. Theoretically, the project will seek to extend collective action theory and provide insights on group functioning, by examining the contexts in which farmer cooperation in production emerges and is sustained. Empirically, the detailed primary data already collected by Agarwal in India, France and Romania will be analysed. In the latter two countries, the surveys were undertaken in collaboration with researchers in Europe and the UK.

Apart from fully analysing this survey material, Agarwal will extend the research to additional countries, especially in Europe and former socialist regimes, where group farming is ongoing. In addition to adding to the body of knowledge through academic publications, this subject has substantial potential for providing policy pointers to governments, international agencies and civil society on ways of improving the viability of smallholder agriculture. The results will thus be disseminated via seminar presentations and workshops.

Agarwal also plans to continue working with researchers and practitioners in the UK and South Asia, on a range of group farms that were catalysed four years ago through an action-research project in eastern India and Nepal. Agarwal's writings influenced aspects of this project in its early stages, and she later provided direct inputs to help shape the farm structures. This project constitutes an unusual opportunity to study the process of institutional change.

Project 2. Gender gaps in property ownership

The issue of women's rights in land and property is now increasingly being recognised across nations as one of key importance for gender equality and economic inclusion, and it is part of the UN's Fifth Sustainable Development Goal. Agarwal pioneered the research on this subject in the late 1980s through her writings, including a multiple award-winning book, *A Field of One's Own: Gender and Land Rights in South Asia* (Cambridge University Press, 1994) covering five countries, and numerous papers. She also led a civil society campaign to amend the Hindu inheritance law in India in 2005, to make it gender equal.

Yet much more remains to be done, both in research and its application. Under the Balzan project, she will work with two early-career colleagues in India on new data sets (including land records) which can enable an all-India analysis of the extent of gender inequality in property, its regional variations, and its implications for food security, poverty alleviation, children's welfare and women's empowerment.

Project 3: Environment and conservation

This project will extend Agarwal's earlier in-depth research on forest conservation and gender in new directions. In particular, she will examine the ways in which the traditional concept of sacred groves is being used by local communities in the Himalayas to create social barriers to deforestation. For this purpose, a field survey and historical research will be undertaken in collaboration with one of her doctoral students, as well as with a mid-career researcher based in a local institution and a senior colleague at the Institute of Economic Growth, Delhi.

PROFILES

THE INTERNATIONAL BALZAN FOUNDATION

The *International Balzan Foundation "Prize"* aims to promote, throughout the world, culture, science, and the most meritorious initiatives in the cause of humanity, peace and fraternity among peoples, regardless of nationality, race or creed. This aim is attained through the annual awarding of prizes in two general academic categories: literature, the moral sciences and the arts; medicine and the physical, mathematical and natural sciences. Specific subjects for the awarding of Prizes are chosen on an annual basis.

Nominations for these prizes are received at the Foundation's request from the world's leading academic institutions. Candidates are selected by the *General Prize Committee*, composed of eminent European scholars and scientists. Prizewinners must allocate half of the Prize to research work involving young researchers. At intervals of not less than three years, the Balzan Foundation also awards a prize of varying amounts for Humanity, Peace and Fraternity among Peoples. The *International Balzan Foundation "Prize"* attains its financial means from the *International Balzan Foundation "Fund"* which administers Eugenio Balzan's estate.

THE ACCADEMIA NAZIONALE DEI LINCEI

The *Accademia Nazionale dei Lincei*, founded in 1603 by the Roman-Umbrian aristocrat Federico Cesi and three other young scholars, Anastasio De Filiis, Johannes Eck and Francesco Stelluti, is the oldest scientific academy in the world. It promotes academic excellence through its Fellows, whose earliest members included Galileo Galilei, among many other renowned names.

The Academy's mission is "to promote, coordinate, integrate and disseminate scientific knowledge in its highest expressions in the context of cultural unity and universality".

The activities of the Academy are carried out according to two guiding principles that complement one another: to enrich academic knowledge and disseminate the fruits of this. To this end, the Accademia Nazionale dei Lincei organises national and international conferences, meetings and seminars, and encourages academic cooperation and exchange between scientists and scholars at the national and international level. The Academy promotes research activities and missions, confers awards and grants, publishes the reports of its own sessions and the notes and records presented therein, as well as the proceedings of its conferences, meetings and seminars.

The Academy further provides – either upon request or on its own initiative – advice to public institutions and drafts relevant reports when appropriate. Since 1992, the Academy has served as an official adviser to the President of the Italian Republic in relation to scholarly and scientific matters.

THE SWISS ACADEMIES OF ARTS AND SCIENCES

The Association of the *Swiss Academies of Arts and Sciences* includes the Swiss Academy of Sciences (SCNAT), the Swiss Academy of Humanities and Social Sciences (SAHS), the Swiss Academy of Medical Sciences (SAMS), and the Swiss Academy of Engineering Sciences (SATW) as well as the two Centres for Excellence TA-SWISS and Science et Cité. Their collaboration is focused on methods of anticipating future trends, ethics and the dialogue between science, the arts and society. It is the aim of the *Swiss Academies of Arts and Sciences* to develop an equal dialogue between academia and society and to advise Government on scientifically based, socially relevant questions. The academies stand for an open and pluralistic understanding of science and the arts. Over the long-term, they mutually commit to resolving interdisciplinary questions in the following areas:

– They offer knowledge and expertise in relation to socially relevant subjects in the fields of Education, Research and Technology.
– They adhere to the concept of ethically-based responsibility in gaining and applying scientific and humanistic knowledge.
– They build bridges between Academia, Government and Society.

AGREEMENTS ON COLLABORATION BETWEEN
THE INTERNATIONAL BALZAN FOUNDATION "PRIZE",
THE ACCADEMIA NAZIONALE DEI LINCEI AND
THE SWISS ACADEMIES OF ARTS AND SCIENCES

(Hereafter referred to as the 'Balzan', the 'Lincei' and the 'Swiss Academies', respectively)

The main points of the agreements between the Balzan, the Swiss Academies and the Lincei are the following:

1) The promotion of the Balzan Prize and the presentation of the Prizewinners through the academies' channels of communication, in Italy and Switzerland as well as abroad. By virtue of the relations of the Swiss Academies and the Lincei with academies of other countries and with international academic organizations, they will contribute to more widespread circulation of news related to the Balzan;

2) On the occasion of the Awards ceremony of the Balzan Prize, held on alternating years in Berne and Rome, each academy will contribute to the academic organization of an interdisciplinary Forum, in the course of which the Prizewinners of that year will present their academic work and discuss it with other academics proposed by the academies. Furthermore, in the years when the ceremony is held in Rome, one of the Prizewinners will give the Annual Balzan Lecture in Switzerland, and when the ceremony is held in Berne, the Annual Balzan Lecture will be organized at the headquarters of the Lincei in Rome;

3) The academies will contribute to a series of publications in English (ideally with summaries in Italian, German and French), created by the Balzan, with the collaboration of the Balzan Prizewinners.

To promote and supervise all these initiatives, two Commissions have been set up, one between the Balzan and the Swiss Academies (at present composed of Antonio Loprieno and Dr. Markus Zürcher) and another between the Balzan and the Lincei (at present composed of Sergio Carrà and Paolo Matthiae). Both commissions are chaired by Professor Alberto Quadrio-Curzio as a representative of the Balzan, which is also represented by Professor Enrico Decleva. The Balzan Secretary General, Dr. Suzanne Werder, has been appointed Secretary of both Commissions.

THE BALZAN FOUNDATION "PRIZE"
BOARD

(2019)

ANTONIO PADOA SCHIOPPA *Member*
Professor Emeritus of Legal History at the University of Milan; former President of the Istituto Lombardo, Academy of Sciences and the Humanities in Milan; Corresponding Foreign Fellow of the Académie des inscriptions et belles-lettres, Institut de France, Paris

LAURA SADIS *Member*
MA (Economics), Swiss Taxation Expert; member of the Assembly of the International Committee of the Red Cross (ICRC); former member of the Swiss National Council; former State Councillor of the Canton Ticino, head of the Department of Financial and Economic Affairs

GENERAL PRIZE COMMITTEE

(2019)

Luciano Maiani

Chairman
Professor Emeritus of Theoretical Physics at the University of Rome "La Sapienza"; Fellow of the Accademia Nazionale dei Lincei, Rome, and of the American Physical Society

Bengt Gustafsson

Vice-Chairman
Professor Emeritus of Theoretical Astrophysics at the University of Uppsala; Member of the Royal Swedish Academy of Sciences, the Royal Danish Academy of Sciences and Letters, and the Norwegian Academy of Science and Letters

Antonio Padoa Schioppa

Vice-Chairman
Professor Emeritus of Legal History at the State University of Milan; former President of the Istituto Lombardo, Academy of Sciences and the Humanities, Milan; Foreign Fellow of the Académie des inscriptions et belles-lettres, Institut de France, Paris

Sierd A.P.L. Cloetingh

Distinguished Utrecht University Professor; President of the Academia Europaea; President of the COST (European Cooperation in Science & Technology) Association; former Vice President of the European Research Council; member of the Royal Netherlands Academy of Arts and Sciences, the Norwegian Academy of Science and Letters, the Royal Danish Academy of Sciences and Letters, the German Academy of Technical Sciences and honorary member of the Hungarian Academy of Sciences

DONATELLA DELLA PORTA	Professor of Political Science, Dean of the Department of Political and Social Sciences and Director of the Centre of Social Movement Studies at the Scuola Normale Superiore in Florence
BØRGE DIDERICHSEN	Former Vice President, Novo Nordisk, Denmark; Chairman of the International Advisory Board of VIB (Flemish Institute of Biotechnology) in Ghent, Belgium
SALWA EL-SHAWAN CASTELO-BRANCO	Professor of Ethnomusicology, Director of the Instituto de Etnomusicologia – Centro de Estudos em Música e Dança, Universidade Nova de Lisboa, Portugal; President of the International Council for Traditional Music
ÉTIENNE GHYS	Permanent Secretary of the Académie des sciences, Institut de France, Paris; Research Director CNRS (Centre National de la Recherche Scientifique), École Normale Supérieure de Lyon
ANDREA GIARDINA	Professor of Roman History at the Scuola Normale Superiore, Pisa; President of the International Committee of Historical Sciences; Fellow of the Accademia Nazionale dei Lincei, Rome
H. CHARLES J. GODFRAY	Professor of Population Biology at the University of Oxford, Director of the Oxford Martin School and Fellow of Jesus College; Fellow of the Royal Society
NATHALIE HEINICH	Research Director in sociology at the Centre National de la Recherche Scientifique (CNRS), Paris; Member of the Centre de Recherches sur les Arts et le Langage (CRAL) at the École des Hautes Études en SciencesSociales (EHESS), Paris
JULES A. HOFFMANN	Distinguished Class Research Director at the Centre National de la Recherche Scientifique (Emeritus), Institute of Molecular and Cellular Biology, Strasbourg; Professor at the University of Strasbourg; former President of the Académie des sciences, Institut de France, Paris; Member of the Académie française; 2011 Nobel Prize for Physiology or Medicine

PETER KUON	Professor of Romance Philology at the University of Salzburg, Austria
THOMAS MAISSEN	Director of the German Historical Institute in Paris; Chair in Early Modern History at the University of Heidelberg; Member of the Heidelberger Academy of Sciences and Humanities
ERWIN NEHER	Director Emeritus, Max Planck Institute for Biophysical Chemistry, Göttingen; Member of the Academia Europaea; Foreign Associate of the US National Academy of Sciences and of the Royal Society, London; 1991 Nobel Prize for Physiology or Medicine
MARJAN SCHWEGMAN	Professor Emeritus of Political and Cultural History of the Twentieth Century, Utrecht University; former Director of the Royal Netherlands Institute in Rome
QUENTIN SKINNER	Barber Beaumont Professor of the Humanities, Queen Mary University of London; Fellow of the British Academy and of the Academia Europaea; Foreign Fellow of the Accademia Nazionale dei Lincei, Rome
VICTOR STOICHITA	Chair of Modern Art History at the University of Fribourg, Switzerland; Foreign Fellow of the Accademia Nazionale dei Lincei, Rome
PETER SUTER	Honorary Professor of Medicine at the University of Geneva; former President of the Swiss Academies of Arts and Sciences
CARLO WYSS	Former Director for Accelerators at CERN. Expert in the design of superconducting acceleration cavities and magnets for series manufacture by industry

STEFAN GERSTER

Member
Dr. iur., LL.M., Certified Specialist SBA Construction and Real Estate Law; Partner of CMS von Erlach Poncet Ltd.; member of the Royal Institution of Chartered Surveyors (MRICS); Lecturer at the University of Zurich, Center for Urban & Real Estate Management (CUREM)

LAURA SADIS

Member
MA (Economics), Swiss Taxation Expert; member of the Assembly of the International Committee of the Red Cross (ICRC); former member of the Swiss National Council; former State Councillor of the Canton Ticino, head of the Department of Financial and Economic Affairs

BALZAN PRIZEWINNERS
FOR LITERATURE, MORAL SCIENCES, AND THE ARTS, FOR PHYSICAL, MATHEMATICAL AND NATURAL SCIENCES, AND MEDICINE

2019
Luigi Ambrosio (Italy) Theory of Partial Differential Equations
Jacques Aumont (France) Film Studies
Michael Cook (USA / UK) Islamic Studies
Research Group: Erika von Mutius, Klaus F. Rabe, Werner Seeger, Tobias Welte – DZL: The German Center for Lung Research (Germany)
    Pathophysiology of respiration: from basic sciences to the bedside

2018
Eva Kondorosi (Hungary / France) Chemical Ecology
Detlef Lohse (The Netherlands / Germany)
Jürgen Osterhammel (Germany) Global History
Marilyn Strathern (UK) Social Anthropology

2017
Bina Agarwal (India / UK) Gender Studies
Aleida and Jan Assmann (Germany) Collective Memory
James P. Allison and Robert D. Schreiber (USA) Immunological Approaches
    in Cancer Therapy
Michaël Gillon (Belgium) The Sun's Planetary System and Exoplanets

2016
Piero Boitani (Italy) Comparative Literature
Federico Capasso (USA / Italy) Applied Photonics
Reinhard Jahn (Germany) Molecular and Cellular Neuroscience
Robert O. Keohane (USA) International Relations: History and Theory

2015
Hans Belting (Germany) History of European Art (1300-1700)
Francis Halzen (Belgium / USA) Astroparticle Physics including neutrino
    and gamma-ray observation
David Michael Karl (USA) Oceanography
Joel Mokyr (USA / Israel) Economic History

2014

Ian Hacking (Canada) Epistemology and Philosophy of Mind
David Tilman (USA) Basic/applied Plant Ecology
Dennis Sullivan (USA) Mathematics (pure/applied)
Mario Torelli (Italy) Classical Archaeology

2013

Alain Aspect (France) Quantum Information Processing and
    Communication
Manuel Castells (USA/Catalonia) Sociology
Pascale Cossart (France) Infectious Diseases: basic and clinical aspects
André Vauchez (France) Medieval History

2012

David Charles Baulcombe (UK) Epigenetics
Ronald M. Dworkin (USA) Jurisprudence
Kurt Lambeck (Australia/The Netherlands) Solid Earth Sciences, with
    emphasis on interdisciplinary research
Reinhard Strohm (UK/Germany) Musicology

2011

Bronislaw Baczko (Switzerland/Poland) Enlightenment Studies
Peter Robert Lamont Brown (USA/Ireland) Ancient History (The Graeco-
    Roman World)
Russell Scott Lande (UK/USA) Theoretical Biology or Bioinformatics
Joseph Ivor Silk (USA/UK) The Early Universe (From the Planck Time to
    the First Galaxies)

2010

Manfred Brauneck (Germany) The History of Theatre in All Its Aspects
Carlo Ginzburg (Italy) European History (1400-1700)
Jacob Palis (Brazil) Mathematics (pure and applied)
Shinya Yamanaka (Japan) Stem Cells: Biology and Potential Applications

2009

Terence Cave (UK) Literature since 1500
Michael Grätzel (Switzerland/Germany) The Science of New Materials
Brenda Milner (Canada/UK) Cognitive Neurosciences
Paolo Rossi Monti (Italy) History of Science

2008

Wallace S. Broecker (USA) The Science of Climate Change
Maurizio Calvesi (Italy) The Visual Arts since 1700
Ian H. Frazer (Australia/UK) Preventive Medicine
Thomas Nagel (USA/Serbia) Moral Philosophy

2007

> ROSALYN HIGGINS (UK) International Law since 1945
> SUMIO IIJIMA (Japan) Nanoscience
> MICHEL ZINK (France) European Literature (1000 1500)
> BRUCE BEUTLER (USA) and JULES HOFFMANN (France/Luxembourg) Innate
> Immunity

2006

> LUDWIG FINSCHER (Germany) History of Western Music since 1600
> QUENTIN SKINNER (UK) Political Thought; History and Theory
> PAOLO DE BERNARDIS (Italy) and ANDREW LANGE (USA) Observational
> Astronomy and Astrophysics
> ELLIOT MEYEROWITZ (USA) and CHRISTOPHER SOMERVILLE (USA/Canada)
> Plant Molecular Genetics

2005

> PETER HALL (UK) The Social and Cultural History of Cities since the
> Beginning of the 16th Century
> LOTHAR LEDDEROSE (Germany) The History of the Art of Asia
> PETER and ROSEMARY GRANT (USA/UK) Population Biology
> RUSSELL HEMLEY (USA) and HO-KWANG MAO (USA/China) Mineral Physics

2004

> PIERRE DELIGNE (USA/Belgium) Mathematics
> NIKKI RAGOZIN KEDDIE (USA) The Islamic World from the End of the 19th
> to the End of the 20th Century
> MICHAEL MARMOT (UK) Epidemiology
> COLIN RENFREW (UK) Prehistoric Archaeology

2003

> REINHARD GENZEL (Germany) Infrared Astronomy
> ERIC HOBSBAWM (UK/Egypt) European History since 1900
> WEN-HSIUNG LI (USA/Taiwan) Genetics and Evolution
> SERGE MOSCOVICI (France/Romania) Social Psychology

2002

> WALTER JAKOB GEHRING (Switzerland) Developmental Biology
> ANTHONY THOMAS GRAFTON (USA) History of the Humanities
> XAVIER LE PICHON (France/Vietnam) Geology
> DOMINIQUE SCHNAPPER (France) Sociology

2001

> JAMES SLOSS ACKERMAN (USA) History of Architecture
> JEAN-PIERRE CHANGEUX (France) Cognitive Neurosciences
> MARC FUMAROLI (France) Literary History and Criticism (post 1500)
> CLAUDE LORIUS (France) Climatology

2000

    ILKKA HANSKI (Finland) Ecological Sciences

    MICHEL MAYOR (Switzerland) Instrumentation and Techniques in
        Astronomy and Astrophysics

    MICHAEL STOLLEIS (Germany) Legal History since 1500

    MARTIN LITCHFIELD WEST (UK) Classical Antiquity

1999

    LUIGI LUCA CAVALLI-SFORZA (USA/Italy) The Science of Human Origins

    JOHN ELLIOTT (UK) History, 1500-1800

    MIKHAEL GROMOV (France/Russia) Mathematics

    PAUL RICŒUR (France) Philosophy

1998

    HARMON CRAIG (USA) Geochemistry

    ROBERT MCCREDIE MAY (UK/Australia) Biodiversity

    ANDRZEJ WALICKI (USA/Poland) The Cultural and Social History of the
        Slavonic World

1997

    CHARLES COULSTON GILLISPIE (USA) History and Philosophy of Science

    THOMAS WILSON MEADE (UK) Epidemiology

    STANLEY JEYARAJA TAMBIAH (USA/Sri Lanka) Social Sciences: Social
        Anthropology

1996

    ARNO BORST (Germany) History: Medieval Cultures

    ARNT ELIASSEN (Norway) Meteorology

    STANLEY HOFFMANN (France/USA/Austria) Political Science:
        Contemporary International Relations

1995

    YVES BONNEFOY (France) Art History and Art Criticism

    CARLO M. CIPOLLA (Italy) Economic History

    ALAN J. HEEGER (USA) The Science of New Non-Biological Materials

1994

    NORBERTO BOBBIO (Italy) Law and Political Science

    RENÉ COUTEAUX (France) Biology

    FRED HOYLE (UK) and MARTIN SCHWARZSCHILD (USA/Germany)
        Astrophysics

1993

WOLFGANG H. BERGER (USA/Germany) Palaeontology with special
   reference to Oceanography
LOTHAR GALL (Germany) History: Societies of the 19th and 20th Centuries
JEAN LECLANT (France) Art and Archaeology of the Ancient World

1992

ARMAND BOREL (USA/Switzerland) Mathematics
GIOVANNI MACCHIA (Italy) History and Criticism of Literature
EBRAHIM M. SAMBA (Gambia) Preventive Medicine

1991

GYÖRGY LIGETI (Austria/Hungary/Romania) Music
VITORINO MAGALHÃES GODINHO (Portugal) History: The Emergence of
   Europe in the 15th and 16th Centuries
JOHN MAYNARD SMITH (UK) Genetics and Evolution

1990

WALTER BURKERT (Switzerland/Germany) The Study of the Ancient World
JAMES FREEMAN GILBERT (USA) Geophysics
PIERRE LALIVE D'EPINAY (Switzerland) Private International Law

1989

EMMANUEL LÉVINAS (France/Lithuania) Philosophy
LEO PARDI (Italy) Ethology
MARTIN JOHN REES (UK) High Energy Astrophysics

1988

SHMUEL NOAH EISENSTADT (Israel/Poland) Sociology
RENÉ ÉTIEMBLE (France) Comparative Literature
MICHAEL EVENARI (Israel/France) and OTTO LUDWIG LANGE (Germany)
   Applied Botany

1987

JEROME SEYMOUR BRUNER (USA) Human Psychology
RICHARD W. SOUTHERN (UK) Medieval History
PHILLIP V. TOBIAS (South Africa) Physical Anthropology

1986

OTTO NEUGEBAUER (USA/Austria) History of Science
ROGER REVELLE (USA) Oceanography/Climatology
JEAN RIVERO (France) Basic Human Rights

1985
>
> Ernst H.J. Gombrich (UK/Austria) History of Western Art
> Jean-Pierre Serre (France) Mathematics

1984
>
> Jan Hendrik Oort (The Netherlands) Astrophysics
> Jean Starobinski (Switzerland) History and Criticism of Literature
> Sewall Wright (USA) Genetics

1983
>
> Francesco Gabrieli (Italy) Oriental Studies
> Ernst Mayr (USA/Germany) Zoology
> Edward Shils (USA) Sociology

1982
>
> Jean-Baptiste Duroselle (France) Social Sciences
> Massimo Pallottino (Italy) Studies of Antiquity
> Kenneth Vivian Thimann (USA/UK) Pure and Applied Botany

1981
>
> Josef Pieper (Germany) Philosophy
> Paul Reuter (France) International Public Law
> Dan Peter McKenzie, Drummond Hoyle Matthews and Frederick John
> Vine (UK) Geology and Geophysics

1980
>
> Enrico Bombieri (USA/Italy) Mathematics
> Jorge Luis Borges (Argentina) Philology, Linguistics and Literary Criticism
> Hassan Fathy (Egypt) Architecture and Urban Planning

1979
>
> Torbjörn Caspersson (Sweden) Biology
> Jean Piaget (Switzerland) Social and Political Science
> Ernest Labrousse (France) and Giuseppe Tucci (Italy) History

1962
>
> Paul Hindemith (Germany) Music
> Andrej Kolmogorov (Russia) Mathematics
> Samuel Eliot Morison (USA) History
> Karl von Frisch (Austria) Biology

BALZAN PRIZEWINNERS
FOR HUMANITY, PEACE AND FRATERNITY
AMONG PEOPLES

2018 TERRE DES HOMMES FOUNDATION - HELPING CHILDREN WORLDWIDE, SIMSONE project: An Innovative Training Model to Save Thousands of Infants and Mothers during Childbirth in the Rural Areas of Mali

2014 VIVRE EN FAMILLE (France), the creation of a maternity unit and the revitalization of a school in Ibambi in the Democratic Republic of the Congo (DRC)

2007 KARLHEINZ BÖHM (Austria/Germany), Organisation *Menschen für Menschen*, Aid for Ethiopia

2004 COMMUNITY OF SANT'EGIDIO, DREAM programme combating AIDS and malnutrition in Mozambique

2000 ABDUL SATTAR EDHI (Pakistan/India)

1996 INTERNATIONAL COMMITTEE OF THE RED CROSS, endeavours in the hospitals of Wazir Akbar Khan and Karte Seh in Kabul, Afghanistan

1991 ABBÉ PIERRE (France)

1986 UNITED NATIONS REFUGEE AGENCY

1978 MOTHER TERESA OF CALCUTTA (India/Macedonia)

1962 H.H. JOHN XXIII (Vatican City/Italy)

1961 NOBEL FOUNDATION

FINITO DI STAMPARE
PER CONTO DI LEO S. OLSCHKI EDITORE
PRESSO ABC TIPOGRAFIA • CALENZANO (FI)
NEL MESE DI MARZO 2021

THE ANNUAL BALZAN LECTURE

1. *The Evolution of Darwin's Finches, Mockingbirds and Flies*, by Peter and Rosemary Grant. 2010

2. *Humanists with Inky Fingers. The Culture of Correction in Renaissance Europe*, by Anthony Thomas Grafton. 2011.

3. *Cognitive Archaeology from Theory to Practice: The Early Cycladic Sanctuary at Keros*, by Colin Renfrew. 2012.

4. *Fair Society, Healthy Lives*, by Michael Marmot. 2013.

5. *Of Moon and Land, Ice and Strand: Sea Level during Glacial Cycles*, by Kurt Lambeck. 2014.

6. *"Far other worlds, and other seas": Thinking with Literature in the Twenty-First Century*, by Terence Cave. 2015.

7. *Thinking about Liberty: An Historian's Approach*, by Quentin Skinner. 2016.

8. *IceCube and the Discovery of High-Energy Cosmic Neutrinos*, by Francis Halzen. 2018.

9. *From Quantum Cascade Lasers to Flat Optics for the Twenty-First Century*, by Federico Capasso. 2019.

10. *Beyond Family Farming: Gendering the Collective*, by Bina Agarwal, 2021.